LIVING WITH AIR PLANTS

Beginners Guide To Understanding Air Plants, Growing Air Plants and Air Plant Care

CALVIN ROBERT

Table of Contents

CHAPTER ONE 3

    INTRODUCTION..3

    AMAZING FACTS ABOUT AIR PLANTS 5

CHAPTER TWO 22

    NICE ENVIRONMENT.....................................22

    AIR PLANT SPECIES..23

CHAPTER THREE 38

    ABOUT AIR PLANT ROOTS...........................38

    Air Plant Life Cycle 43

    Care for Air Plants in Aeriums or Terrariums 45

    THERE ARE MANY TYPES OF INDOOR AIR PLANTS..50

CHAPTER FIVE 54

    SKY PLANT (TILLANDSIA IONANTHA) 54

    CONCLUSION...87

    Growing Conditions 88

    THE END 94

CHAPTER ONE

INTRODUCTION

The Tillandsia or Air Plants are easy to care for. However, they require proper environmental considerations and care. They are known as "air plants" because they don't need soil, but they still require light, water, nutrients and light to survive. Technically, air plants are epiphytes. This means that they can grow in nature on another tree or host. They do not steal nutrients from the host and only use it as a place to grow. To capture moisture and nutrients from the air, air plants use tiny vessels called trichos located in their leaves. They don't need soil, and most Tillandsia shouldn't be planted in soil. This allows them to thrive in many different environments, vessels, and spaces. Air plants can be used in many different situations, which has led to an increase in popularity of Tillandsia decorations for homes or offices. Although air plants are easy to grow, they require care to live healthy lives. Tillandias can live many years if they are well cared for and even produce "pups", which will provide years of enjoyment.

AMAZING FACTS ABOUT AIR PLANTS

Air plants are unique and beautiful houseplants that don't require soil. These plants are a great choice for those with black thumbs, such as me! Anyone who is looking for a brightening touch to their home without the need to water or repot weekly. These are some great facts about air plants you should know.

The air plants (Tillandsia) are fascinating and one the most loved houseplants. Did you know they can survive in many different conditions? Whether you're new to growing air plants, or have been gardening for years, there are always new things to learn. These plants are ideal for indoor gardening and are easy to maintain. We will be sharing ten incredible facts about air plants. What are some amazing facts about the Air Plant? Air plants can survive in soil. But did you know that they can also be grown upside down? The purification of the air around them is a hallmark of air plants. They can remove toxins from furniture, such as formaldehyde. They can even change their color and release oxygen at night. There are many types of air plants. They come in so many colors it's hard to resist one.

1. They can grow without soil

Although most plants rely on soil to provide nutrients, air plants can absorb nutrients and moisture from the air through their leaves. Because of the natural structure and function of their roots, this feat is possible. Air plants will happily absorb nutrients from driftwood, sea sponges, and some rocks.

2. They use CAM Photosynthesis

A special form of photosynthesis is used by air plants, crassulacean acids metabolism (CAM). The CAM process allows for efficient water use by allowing the plant to only open its stomata during nighttime when it is cooler. C-CAM is the most common method of opening stomata during day and night.

Many succulents, including air plants use P-CAM (Phosphoenolpyruvate Catalase) which means that they only open the stomata at night. This allows air plants more oxygen at night.

3. You can grow in a variety of climates

Air plants don't have any special requirements regarding temperature and humidity. Air plants can thrive in a variety of climates such as desert-like environments and humid rainforest habitats.

It is easy to grow air plants. They can be found almost anywhere in the world. There are many places where you can find air plants, including South Africa, Australia, and Mexico. Air plants can survive in many climates, including the Mediterranean, Europe, and Central America. Air plants can be grown anywhere in the world.

4. After blooming, air plants grow offsets (Pups).

There is a good chance that your air plant has already begun to produce pups, or "offsets" as they are commonly known. It is extremely simple to propagate them as all you need to do is to allow them to grow, then cut them off. As long as one plant survives there will always be another.

You can take them out and place them anywhere they will thrive.

This makes air plants extremely useful for people who need to quickly fill large spaces. You only need one plant. Once it begins to grow pups, you can remove them and place them anywhere they will thrive.

5. Pineapples Are Very Closely Related to Air Plants

Although it might seem contrary at first, air plants are part of the pineapple family. Bromeliads include both pineapples and air plants. Because each plant uses bromeliads in a unique way, they look very different. The leaves of the pineapple plant absorb water, while those of us who are air plants absorb moisture from the surrounding environment.

6. Air plants are not toxic to pets or children

Air plants are safe for both humans and animals. There are no known toxicities in air plants so your children can play with them and even chew on the leaves. They are a great choice if you have pets or children who are interested in plants. Air plants are able to absorb nutrients and water from the environment, rather than ingesting it like other plants. This eliminates the need for toxic fertilizers entering their systems.

7. Air Plants Can Change Colors

The environment in which they live can affect the color of their plants. There is a possibility that your air plant might change color as the environment changes. You can find them growing in many colors, including pink, orange, and light green or yellow. You can find them growing in many colors, including pink, orange, and light green or yellow. They can change their colors easily due to the way that air plants use photosynthesis in its leaves and petals. These parts begin to absorb sunlight and transform it into energy for the plant. This can cause changes in color depending on the amount of exposure.

8. They bloom near the end of their lives

The first sign that an air plant is about to die is when it starts blooming. Most plants will eventually stop growing and become smaller once this happens. Only the final stages of air plants bloom.

The last stages of an air plant's life are when they bloom. If they start to open up, it is likely that they will not live long. If they are still healthy, you may be able save them by moving the container to a more shaded area in your home or office.

9. Air plants are epiphytes and can also be lithothetes

Air plants tend to grow on large, non-living objects when they are in the wild. If you want to replicate the same effect at your home, you can place them between stones and other materials. It will grow fine as long as it gets sunlight and has water. This is why air plants are a great choice for people who want to have a low-maintenance, low-maintenance option.

10. Anyone Can Get a "Green Thumb" from Air Plants

Are you afraid of gardening houseplants because you don't have a green thumb. An air plant can prove you wrong. They are easy to grow and maintain. They don't require any fertilization or watering, and will grow just fine in your home. Air plants can survive without much light. Your plant will grow happily as long as it gets some indirect sunlight. It should be placed where it can get some indirect sunlight. This will allow your plant to thrive. You will need one air plant, a glass container that has water inside it and a glass container to hold the water. Place your air plants near a window so they get sunlight every day. Watch them grow and thrive over time.

11. An Air Plant that is in a bind can be easily resurrected

An air plant that is about to die doesn't have to be thrown out. If your plant starts to wilt or turn brown, you can place your dying plant inside a container of water. Then, put that container in a larger container or jar. Cover the top. This will allow your plant more humidity. This process can be done for approximately ten days. If you are happy with the results, move your growing air plants into a smaller container that has some soil. You can allow them to grow new roots and, once they have grown enough, you will be able separate them from their air plant containers. Air plants aren't just small plants you can decorate your house or office with. These plants have amazing properties that set them apart from other plants. These incredible facts will allow you to learn more about these plants and their popularity. Many people start air plants because it is rewarding to receive pups after their original plant dies. It is common for people to have more than one plant once they have it. Although these plants might seem unlikely gifts, they can bring life and color to your home.

CHAPTER TWO

NICE ENVIRONMENT

Your environment is the most important thing to think about when caring for air plants. Although we have provided a list of general tips for air plant care, you should also consider the environment when choosing watering frequency and method. You might need to water your plants more often if you live in a dry climate. If your plants are located in an area that receives high humidity, they may require less watering.

AIR PLANT SPECIES

There are many species of Tillandsia. Each one is unique in its shape, size and growth patterns. Although most Tillandsia will be able to use the same care tips, it is important to take into account the specific needs of each individual Tillandsia. Silver-leaved plants, and those with higher trichome concentrations, will thrive with more light and less water. Darker green plants, however, will need more water and may be more vulnerable to sun damage.

Light

Light is essential for all living creatures, including air plants. You will need to ensure that your indoor plants are within easy reach of a sufficient light source. You can place them within 3 to 5 feet of a window or close to an artificial light source. Avoid letting your air plants see too much sun. This can cause damage, even in indoor environments. If your plants are outside, ensure they are kept in shade and not exposed to full sunlight. Only a few varieties can withstand direct sunlight. Place your air plants in the bathroom or kitchen window. The steam/moisture will keep you happy. As long as plants are not too far away from artificial light, and get enough light per day, artificial light can be used as a source of sufficient light.

What amount of light do air plants need?

Air plants are very easy to maintain, which is a great thing.

They are not maintenance-free. However, they can still be affected by light, water, and air. Tillandsias, also known as air plants, prefer bright but indirect filtered light. As these windows receive more indirect light, we recommend that they face either north or south. We have experimented with various air plants in our home and found that the ones that do well are located near our kitchen window. This is partly shaded by trees outside so that they receive plenty of natural light. Your environment's humidity can have an impact on how much light your plants can take. Your air plants will tolerate a little more sun if they are in a humid environment. They will also not dry out as quickly. Air plants that live outside in a humid Florida environment may be able to tolerate more sunlight. However, most air plants are not suited for full or direct sun. Air plants are great office plants because they need indirect light. They can either get light from a window or artificially from full-spectrum fluorescent lights. There are always exceptions, just like in nature.

Some silver-leafed plants can take more direct sunlight. One of the few tillandsias capable of taking full sunlight is the Xerographica plant. To see how your plants respond to different lighting conditions, we recommend you try placing them in different positions. What areas have you seen your plants flourish the most? What lighting did NOT work for your air plants?

Water

Let the plants sit face down in a container, bowl or sink for between 10-20 minutes. You should always gently shake off any water that has accumulated on the base of your plants. This can lead to rot or damage to the plants. We recommend watering your plants every morning and letting them dry in their containers for at least 4 hours. Your air plants should never be left in the water for too long. You can also water your air plants by using the "dunking", which involves dipping the plants in water several times and then gently shaking off any excess.

If your plant seems "hungry" or is in distress, you can place them in a bowl for a longer soak. Healthy air plants will have large, open leaves. A dehydrated plant will have curled and closed leaves. It is best to not submerge the flower or bloom as this can cause it to rot. Tap water should be left to cool for at least 24 hours before you water your plants. It is best to use rainwater, pond, or aquarium water whenever possible. You can use spring and bottle water, but not distilled or softened water. Each plant variety will need different watering requirements. It is a bad idea to put your air plants in soil.

Air

Your Air Plant's other important variable is, you guessed it, air! To survive and thrive, the plants need clean air circulation. After watering, it is important to allow the plants to dry in 4 hours. Although Air Plants can be kept in containers, they should not be stored in them. Plants too close to A/C vents could dry out quicker and need more frequent hydration.

Terrariums & Globes

If you plan to keep your air plants indoors in a globe or terrarium, you will need remove them for normal watering. Also, make sure the plant is allowed to dry completely before you leave it out. It should dry for at least 4 hours. You can mist the tillandsia when it is still in its terrarium. You will need to mist your plants less frequently if the globe is smaller or more compact. You can spray the plants with a water mister once a week if your terrarium has more air circulation and is larger. You must ensure that the plant doesn't get too misted and that it dries out within a few hours after being placed in the terrarium.

Sea Urchins

You will need to ensure that the sea urchin kit you purchased has the air plant removed before soaking. The plant should be left out of the sea urchin for several days until it dries completely. The sea urchin will not allow you to return the plant while it is still damp. As the plant's base will become swollen and eventually die, you will cause damage to the air plant. You can mist the sea urchin lightly while it is still wet.

Temperature

Air plants can be found at a variety of temperatures but they are most commonly between 50 and 90 degrees Fahrenheit. You should ensure your plants are protected indoors if you live in freezing areas.

Fertilizer

Bromeliad fertilizer is only needed once per month and can be used in small amounts. Orchid fertilizer can be used in small quantities. You should not over fertilize air plants.

Trimming

Your air plants will eventually grow new leaves and lose some. You can trim any dead or brown leaves from your plants with scissors. After trimming, angle the ends of the leaf to give it a natural appearance. Many air plant varieties ship with the roots intact. You can remove them if you wish. The roots are only used to attach the plant to the host. They can be left on the plant or used to secure your display with hot glue or superglue.

Puppy

Your air plant will start to produce "pups" as it matures and goes through its bloom cycle. The pup can be removed when it is about 1/3 the size of its mother or left on to form a "clump". A "clump" of air plants can be hung on a string. It will impress everyone as it continues to bloom and grows!

CHAPTER THREE

ABOUT AIR PLANT ROOTS

Tillandsia or air plants are part of the epiphyte family. This means they can anchor themselves to another plant, but are not parasitic. This epiphyte classification is available for ferns, Tillandsia (and all Bromeliads), orchids, moss, and most other lichens. These plants are often found on the trunks and branches of tropical rainforest trees, which allows them to receive filtered sunlight from the tree's canopy.

These epiphytes receive all the nutrients they need through their leaves, including sunlight, water, and any organic matter. Tillandsia don't use their roots as a source of nutrients. They only use them as an anchor. Because of the intense competition for light, water and nutrients in densely populated tropical rainforests over the years, epiphytes have evolved and adapted to not require roots. Because they are epiphytes, air plants don't need soil to thrive. This adaptation allows them live in higher places in the rainforest's upper stories that other plants cannot reach. These moisture-rich tree canopies also allow air plants to absorb nutrients from the atmosphere through their trichomes. While that may sound interesting, what should you do with their roots? Their roots will grow and remain untouched , but you can trim them to make them more attractive. You should not cut too close to the base of the plant as this could cause damage. Their roots can be used to attach the plant to driftwood, wreaths, or hanging planters. After they attach to the wood using their roots, they will be able to hold them in position. Air plants can be placed anywhere that has good air flow and indirect light. They can be placed in a glass globe to create living art or sent in a adorable little seashell gift to friends across the country.

Does My Air Plant Get Enough Water?

Leaf tips that turn brown or become crispy are signs of an under-watered air plant. Under-watering can cause the natural concave shape and appearance of air plant leaves to become more exaggerated. It's usually too late to save an air plant if it has been neglected. If the bottom of your plant becomes brown or black and the leaves fall out, it's likely that your plant has succumbed. When it comes to temperature, air plants are quite easygoing. They thrive between 50 and 90 degrees F. Ideal overnight temperatures are about 10 degrees lower than the daytime temperature. A great way to keep your orchids happy is to include Bromeliad or orchid fertilizer in your watering schedule once or twice per month. Add a little to your water, and you can continue as normal. Fertilizing an air plant will encourage it to bloom and reproduce.

Air Plant Life Cycle

Did you know that most air plants only flower once in their lives? These blossoms can last anywhere from a few days up to several months depending on what species they are. They come in a variety of bright colors like red, purple, and pink. The peak of an air plant's life cycle is flowering. However, it also signals the start of a plant's old age. After the flower, the plant will eventually die. But don't despair! Depending on the species, just before, during, or after flowering, your air plant will produce 2-8 "pups." These tiny baby air plants will eventually become their mother plants. When they are about 1/3 to 1/2 their size, pups can be safely separated from their mother plants. You should not remove them too soon, as they are receiving nutrients from the mother plant.

Care for Air Plants in Aeriums or Terrariums

Although larger plants can be placed on a tabletop or windowsill, we also love to include smaller plants in our living art. In fact, our aeriums are a special type of terrarium that is exclusively for air plants. Here are some tips for caring for glass air plants. You can take your air plant out of its glass container by following these steps:

• Follow the above care instructions. Simply remove the plant from the terrarium, aerium or glass and mist/soak the water. After drying, place it back in the glass.

- Remember that glass vessels can create a microclimate. Glass vessels are more humid than surrounding areas.

- Be careful not to place glass vessels too close by a window. The sun's rays are intensified by glass. Your plant shouldn't be fried!

You cannot take your air plant out of its glass container.

- Because your plant will not come out of the glass, it won't be possible to soak it. You'll have to rely on misting instead. This is perfectly fine.

- Because of the smaller glass, there is less air circulation and therefore a longer drying time for plants = less frequent misting.

- Larger glass means more air circulation and less drying time for plants = frequent misting.

- Misting an air plant is best done around it, not inside. It is important to not overwater your air plant, but to provide a humid environment.

- We recommend misting your vessel once a week, then adjusting as needed.

Are air plants able to bloom?

Houseplant owners who are able to properly care for their plants will often be gifted with flowers. Most Tillandsia species only bloom once in their lives. The bloom spikes may be white, pink, purple or red and occur usually in the spring or late winter. Air plants can also produce offsets (or young daughters plants, called pups) around the time they are in bloom. These offsets can be separated from the mother plant by twisting, cutting or tearing them. When the young offset is about half the size of its mother, move it to a different location. Air plants can be neglected, but that doesn't make them easy to ignore. For many years, you will be able to enjoy these little plants.

THERE ARE MANY TYPES OF INDOOR AIR PLANTS

Air plants are any of approximately 500 species of flowering perennial plants from the Tillandsia Genus, which is part of the family. Their roots do not require soil. They extract moisture from the air. These plants are called epiphytes and include Spanish moss. They thrive in their natural environment, which is warm, dry regions that receive bright, filtered sunlight. Air plants grow on trees that are anchored to the bark. They can be grown in an indoor greenhouse, but they are not perennials in warm climates. Air plants were once uncommon in commercial usage, but they are very fashionable and can be used in many hanging garden applications. Although some species can be grown in a pot, others are best mounted on bark or driftwood and suspended from the air. Hanging grids are a great way to display air plants. They can be grouped together and provide good air circulation. You can now find air plants at most garden centers. They are very small and should be seen close up to fully appreciate them. There are many Tillandsia species, but not all have the same name. They are often grouped together as "sky plants" or "air plants". They may also be sold by their species names. These 25 indoor plant types are suitable for indoor gardening, regardless of their name. Because most air plants don't grow in soil, they require special watering. A light misting of water two to three times per week is enough to keep your plants hydrated. This is especially important in dry climates and areas with dry winter air. If your air plant starts to look dry, you can submerge it in the sink overnight to help it thrive again. You can rinse your air plant under running water if it is still in bloom.

CHAPTER FIVE

SKY PLANT (TILLANDSIA IONANTHA)

Tillandsia is a very popular type of air plant. There are many cultivars, but the main species is extremely popular due to its hardiness and resistance to disease. The plant is very attractive. It has layers of silvery-green foliage that turn to shades of red and pink as the plants grow. This color change occurs right before the violet blossoms appear.

Native Area: Mexico Central America, South America

USDA Growing Areas: 9-11

Height: 6-12 Inches

Sun Exposure: Bright, indirect light

'Druid' Sky Plant (Tillandsia. ionantha: 'Druid')

Air plants are becoming more popular and growers are now focusing on unusual colors. The leaves of the Druid cultivar have a peachy pink tone and flowers that are white, unlike the red of the species Tillandsia Ionantha.

Although this plant is small, it is very eye-catching.

Native Area: Mexico Central America, South America

USDA Growing Areas: 9-11

Height: 2 to 4 inches

Sun Exposure: Bright, indirect light

'Maxima' Sky Plant (Tillandsia ionantha Maxima' or 'Huamelula')

The 'Maxima' Sky Plant, also known by 'Huamelula', is worth looking if you are in search of an air plant that will make an impact.

This plant can withstand stronger sun than other air plants and it produces multiple flowers at once. Before the leaves turn coral, they are adorned with stunning purple flowers. This cultivar can reach 5-6 inches high and spread to 3-4 inches.

Native Area: Mexico Central America, South America

USDA Growing Areas: 9-11

Height: 5-6 Inches

Sun Exposure Full sun to partial shade. It does well under fluorescent lights

'Fuego' Sky Plant (Tillandsia ionantha Fuego)

Although tiny, Fuego is quite the show-off. This cultivar was bred to continue blushing even after it has bloomed. They retain their bright green color for many months. Although they are small plants that grow only 1 inch tall, they can quickly fill out. This type of air plant could become a focal point for your collection or be used as a conversation starter at your table.

Native Area - Mexico Central America, South America

USDA Growing Areas: 9-11

Height: 1/2-3 Inches

Sun Exposure: Bright, indirect light

Pink Quill (Tillandsia Cynea)

It is easy to see why Tillandsia Cyanea is called the pink quill. The pink bracts are shaped like feathers and the purple flowers poke out from the sides. This species can be grown in soil, unlike most other air plants. It can live without soil, but it will thrive if it gets plenty of moisture.

Native Area: Ecuador

USDA Growing Areas: 9-11

Height: 8-12 Inches

Sun Exposure: Bright, indirect light

Mad Pupper (Tillandsia aeranthos bergeri)

Tillandsia Aeranthos Berrieni - which we like to call Mad Pupper- is one of the most loved air plants due to its bright flowers. The blooms are spiky pink or blue and they come back every spring. This species is very easy to maintain and prefers bright indirect light or fluorescent lighting.

Native Area: South America

USDA Growing Areas: 9-11

Height: 6-10 Inches

Sun Exposure Indirect, bright light that works well under fluorescent lights

Kolbii' (Tillandsia. scaposa)

Many air plants can grow in strange directions or sideways. The 'Kolbii', which is tall and upright, grows in tight clusters, looking like a bunch of celery. Although it isn't a large plant, the soft gray fuzz of its leaves makes it stand out. This is especially true when they bloom pink. This variety can be classified in many ways like other air plants, including Tillandsia Kolbii, T. scaposa "Kolbii", or T. inonanta var. scaposa.

Native Area: Guatemala

USDA Growing Areas: 9-11

Height: 2-5 Inches

Sun Exposure: Bright, indirect light

Brachycaulos (Tillandsia brachycaulos)

The leaves of the brachycaulos brachycaulos (Tillandsia brachycaulos) spread out from a central growth point. As it gets ready for bloom, the plant turns red. Sometimes, you may find plants that have had their leaves dyed red to appear flowering. The plant is typically small, measuring approximately 3 inches tall with a spread of 4 inches. However, some cultivars can grow larger. One hybrid, brychycaulosx color is bred to stay bright green.

Native Area: Mexico, Central America, Venezuela

USDA Growing Areas: 9-11

Height: 2-8 Inches

Sun Exposure: Bright, indirect light

Bulbous Air plant (Tillandsia bulbsa)

Tillandsia bulbsa gets its common name from the bulbous roots. However, it is the constrained, narrow leaves that are most interesting. Bulbous Air Plants look like tentacles. The leaves will turn purple or red just before they are ready to flower. Tillandsia bulbsosa can be grown outside and has a symbiotic relationship to ants. The bulbs are hollow and the ants live inside them. The ants' waste is then fed to the plant.

Native Area - South America, Central America, South America

USDA Growing Areas: 9-11

Height: 4-7 Inches

Sun Exposure Bright, indirect or partial shade

Cacticola (Tillandsia cacticola)

Cacticola (Tillandsia Cactucola) can be difficult to grow because it doesn't produce many offsets. This air plant is highly valued for its beautiful lavender flowers. The rosette is silvery-green and has leaves that are about 8-9 inches high. From the stem, the flower hangs from the stem. Its habit of growing on cacti is what gives it its name.

Native Area: Peru

USDA Growing Areas: 9-11

Height: 3-9 Inches

Sun Exposure: Bright, indirect light

'Peach' Air Plant (Tillandsia capitata 'Peach')

The thick leaves of Tillandsia capita "Peach" are surprising soft to the touch. As they get ready to flower, they form a silver-green roset that turns to a peachy pink hue. The striking contrast between the purple flower and the peach color is made by their peach coloring. Although the largest plants can reach 5-8 inches in height, 2-3 inch plants are quite common.

Native Area - Mexico and Honduras. Cuba, Dominican Republic.

USDA Growing Areas: 9-11

Height: 2-8 Inches

Sun Exposure Indirect, bright light. Will tolerate full sun

Circinata (Tillandsia circinata)

Tillandsia circuminata has thick silvery-green foliage that give it a substantial appearance. It almost looks like an bulb of or fennel . Although they are only 1 inch at the base, Circinata plants can flower in yellow or purple. They grow to 6-8 inches tall.

Native Area: Mexico, Costa Rica, Bahamas

USDA Growing Areas: 10-11

Height: 6-8 Inches

Sun Exposure Bright, indirect or partial shade

'Cotton Candy' (Tillandsia stricta x T. recurvifolia 'Cotton Candy')

"Cotton Candy" is a hybrid from Tillandsia strictlyaand T. Recurvifolia. Its silvery, long leaves look like a loose spider dahlia. It is known for its pink flower spike. The bracts appear to be inflated. To flower well, this air plant variety requires bright sunlight.

Native area: Hybrid nursery; parents species are native to South America

USDA Growing Areas: 9-11

Height: 5-6 Inches (12 Inches is possible)

Sun Exposure: Bright, indirect light

Loliacea (Tillandsia loliacea)

Loliacea (Tillandsia LOLiacea) is a charming miniature air plant. Although the plant is only 1 1/2 inches tall, it can reach its flower stalks up to 2-3 inches for tiny yellow flowers. These tiny air plants can be found perched on wooden boards or in clusters in terrariums where they can absorb excess moisture.

Native Area: Bolivia, Brazil, Argentina

USDA Growing Areas: 9-11

Height: 1-3 Inches

Sun Exposure: Bright, indirect light

Didsticha (Tillandsia didsticha)

Didsticha (Tillandsia doisticha) is very tall for a Tillandsia and can grow to 1 foot at maturity. The plant's base forms a dense spray of gray-green, slender leaves. The flower stalk emerges from them with small white flowers and pinkish bracts. Burnt Fingers is a popular cultivar.

Native Area: Bolivia, Brazil

USDA Growing Areas: 9-11

Height: 6-12 Inches

Sun Exposure: Bright, indirect light

Dyeriana (Tillandsia dyeriana)

The bright orange inflorescence of dyeriana (Tillandsia Dyeriana) has a tropical vibe. Although the actual flowers are white, the bracts make them stand out. This is one of few air plants that can also grow in pots. It can be more assured of getting adequate moisture. It can grow to 12-18 inches tall when potted. This air plant needs humidity.

Native Area: Mexico, Central America, Ecuador

USDA Growing Zones - 10-11

Height: 3-12 Inches

Sun Exposure: Bright, indirect light

Giant Air Plant (Tillandsia faciculata)

Tillandsia faciculata is a unique air plant. It has many common names. These include the giant, quill-leaf, cardinal, wild, and cardinal. This is the most widely grown of all air plants. There are many varieties and hybrids. This species is attractive for many weeks because of its red-green inflorescence. Native Area Mexico Central America, West Indies and northern South America

USDA Growing Areas: 9-11

Height: up to 3 feet

Sun Exposure: Bright, indirect light

Flabellata (Tillandsia flabellata)

Instead of a rosette with thin leaves, Tillandsia Flabellata is taller and more vase-shaped. It also has a spray of red flowers spikes, which are sometimes called a candelabra. Flabellata, as air plants go is very large and can grow up to 12 inches tall.

Native Area: Mexico Central America

USDA Growing Areas: 9-11

Height: 6-12 Inches

Sun Exposure: Bright, indirect light

Argentea (Tillandsia Fuchsii) var. garcilis)

Formerly known as Tillandsia argentea the argentea plant is a bulbous, pincushion-shaped, argentea airplant with long, thin, gray-green leaves. Tillandsia Fuchsiivar. garcilis, a delicate plant, only grows to about 5-6 inches in height and is 1-2 inches wide. Even the bright orange-red inflorescences are delicate.

Native Region: Mexico. Guatemala. Cuba. Jamaica

USDA Growing Areas: 9-11

Height: 5-6 Inches

Sun Exposure: Bright, indirect light

Funkiana (Tillandsia funkiana)

These long-leafed air plants can bend and curl into unusual shapes, sometimes spiraling around itself. Funkiana (Tillandsia Funkiana), a small species, is ideal for a terrarium, or as a desktop plants. The leaves turn red when the plant is ready to bloom, as with many other air plant varieties. The inflorescence has yellow flowers and is also red.

Native Area: Venezuela

USDA Growing Areas: 9-11

Height: 1-2 Inches

Sun Exposure: Bright, indirect light

Gardneri (Tillandsia gardneri)

Gardneri (Tillandsia garneri) looks a lot like a small or yucca . It has pale grayish leaves and taper to a point. This is a taller air plant that can grow up to 12 inches in height. If you don't have the right conditions for air plants, this species is a great choice. Although it is very forgiving, it still requires plenty of moisture.

Native Area: Trinidad and Tobago (Colombia, eastern Brazil, Venezuela)

USDA Growing Areas: 9-11

Height: 4-12 Inches

Sun Exposure: Bright, indirect light

Ball Moss (Tillandsia Recurvata).

Tillandsia is also known as small ball moss. The nest is more like a nest, with many slender, arching, gray-green leaves. It also has a tall, lavender flower spike. It is a common air plant that naturalizes in the Southeastern United States. The unusual habit of this plant is to allow its seeds to germinate in their seed pods while they are still inside. It is very easy to propagate.

Native area: Southeastern U.S.A, Central America and Chile to northern Argentina

USDA Growing Areas: 9-11

Height: 2-6 Inches

Sun Exposure: Bright, indirect light

'Pink Bronze' (Tillandsia stricta 'Pink Bronze')

A typical pineapple-type roseette of leaves, "Pink Bronze" will develop a hint pinky-bronze color if it is exposed to bright, strong light. The show-stealing flowers are the large, pink-colored purple flowers. This plant can be used as a single specimen in teardrop terrariums.

Native Area: Trinidad and Tobago, South America

USDA Growing Areas: 9-11

Height: 6-12 Inches

Sun Exposure: Bright, indirect light

'Whitestar' (Tillandsia.ixioides.x T..recurvifolia.' Whitestar)

Whitestar is a cross between Tillandsia.ixioides (T.) and T. However, recurvifolia is much bigger than either parent. The bracts are a rose pink color with flowers that range from yellow to cream. Its silver-gray leaves curl giving it movement.

Native area: Nursery hybrid. Parents species are native to South America

USDA Growing Areas: 9-11

Height: 6-12 Inches

Sun Exposure: Bright, indirect light

Xerographica (Tillandsia xerographica)

Xerographica (Tillandsia) is an unusually large, flat, gray-green air plant that curls like a ribbon. The rosette's center produces thinner leaves, but the larger outer leaves make for a striking contrast when grouped with smaller air plants. Curling leaves can be caused by withholding water

Native Area: Mexico Central America

USDA Growing Areas: 9-11

Height: 6-15 Inches

Sun Exposure Indirect, bright light. Will tolerate some direct sunlight

CONCLUSION

There are approximately 500 species of tillandsia. The most well-known is the Spanish Moss, which gracefully drapes from oaks in the American South. This huge genus, which is the largest in the bromeliads family, can sometimes be divided into two groups: the grey-leaved terrestrial plants and the green-leaved moss-covered terrestrial plants. All tillandsia, in fact, are epiphytic air plants. They grow by clinging on to trees and taking excess moisture from the atmosphere. Tillandsia was once rare. They are now more common in garden centers and often sold as part of hanging gardens. Only a handful of tillandsias are allowed to be grown in pots. All others must be mounted.

Growing Conditions

Light Bright, but not direct sunlight. Perfect for this is a south, east, or west window. You can also grow them under fluorescent tubes.

Water: water 2 to 4 times per week with a mister Mist every day if your environment is dry. You should water the plant until it is fully saturated.

Temperature: Some varieties are able to withstand temperatures as low as 0F, but most can thrive between 70 F-85 F. High humidity is an advantage.

Support Glue tillandsias (cork, coral, stone or driftwood) to glue tillandsias. Only a few varieties are able to adapt to soil.

Fertilizer Use a low-copper liquid fertiliser that is diluted to 1/4 strength. Feed your plants once a month.

Propagation

Tillandsias reproduce through the release of offsets (or pups) from the mother plant. The pups can be separated and mounted when they are half the size as the mother. Although you can grow Tillandsias from seeds, it is slow and may take many years.

Mounting

Tillandsias like to be mounted on a hard substrate that doesn't retain water. The option to glue the tillandsia directly onto the substrate is either to use a strong adhesive or to wire it to the base. The plant's base should not be covered with moss, as it could rot. Tillandsia can grow on any decorative mount you want, such as shells, rocks or slate. For maximum effect, group them in decorative clusters. T. T. lindenii and cyanea can be adapted to soil.

Varieties

There are hundreds of species in tillandsia. T. ionantha and T. xerographica are some of the most popular. T. usneoides is the Spanish moss. There are no differences in the growing requirements of different species. T. cyanea, and T.lindenii are two varieties that can be grown in soil and are commonly sold under the "Pink Quill" label. Others species are less adaptable.

Grower's Tips

Tillandsias are a wonderful plant that can bring joy to the garden. Their leaves often bloom in stunning colors. A well-kept collection looks like a healthy coral reef. Overfertilizing and not giving enough water are two of the most common mistakes with tillandsia. The plant will likely be gasping for water if the leaves curl under. It will return to you if you place it in the sink. They require fresh air like epiphytic orchids. Don't over-suffocate them with moss.

THE END